JULIA REVIVES LATIN WITH THE OLYMPIANS

A Latin novella

Taryn Boonpongmanee

Printed in the United States of America.

First Edition.

Cover page designed by Khrunood Art Teach.

Illustrations designed by Thippawan Pengput.

ISBN 979-8-3509-1704-8

www.launchingloveforlatin.com

"As long as you live, keep learning to live."

- LUCIUS ANNAEUS SENECA

PRAFATIO

Freshman year, my teacher asked us to introduce ourselves with our name, grade, and years of Latin experience. Several of my classmates mentioned having 3 or 4 years of experience, often from studying at private schools. I questioned how to introduce myself with my 3 months of Latin experience, most learned from Googling online. I'm from a small town where most believe that Latin is a dead language without applications to daily life, and as a result local school curriculums do not include Latin.

My curiosity about Latin started when I saw Latin words on buildings and monuments. I wanted to know what they said and what they meant. My public elementary school didn't offer any language opportunities and my local middle school had a singular Spanish class that was only open to 2 periods of classes, for a school of 800 kids. Fortunately, my high school gave me the opportunity to explore this curiosity and try Latin. Before I began high school three years ago, I searched online and found free beginner Latin resources. I really enjoyed figuring out and learning Latin on my own from YouTube and online resources. However, it was hard to get further than a certain point due to limited resources in my town.

To promote literacy, accessibility and equality in the field of Classics, I've since started a Latin blog called Launching Love for Latin and a recurring Latin camp in my hometown. During past sessions, it has been so exciting to see waves of enthusiastic young students. There has been so much interest, from across multiple towns in the area, that we've sold out every time and opened up waiting lists for the future. The experience of designing my own curriculum and interacting with eager young students has been incredibly rewarding. I always welcome student feedback, and every session several students have said that they loved learning about gods and goddesses and their origin stories and myths. When creating my own curriculum within these workshops, I hope to always leave my students with a memorable learning experience, and I would like to cater to their interests further. This book serves as an introduction into the magical myths of the ancient world and intends to spark interest in continuing Classics as students enter middle and high school programs. The English version is meant to captivate young learners and the Latin version serves as a fun intermediate Latin book to familiarize students with both the language and myths of the ancient world.

This book is a result of my passion for learning, teaching, and spreading Latin. My love for myths and the gods started with the Percy Jackson series and continued as I read Ovid's *Metamorphoses*. The Olympians fascinate many younger learners, reminding me of myself. My goal is to continue increasing Latin's accessibility for students who, like myself, are interested in understanding one of the cultures whose influence still underpins many of our systems today. I want to change the mindset that Latin is an elitist language and instead use the motion to redefine the diversity and elitism of the field as a way to invite many voices into the conversation of Classics.

I would like to thank Deerfield Academy and my teachers, Dr. Houston and Ms. Delwiche for always supporting my Classics endeavors, as well as the Center for Service and Global Citizenship for awarding me with a grant that has enabled me to write and publish this story. Thank you to my parents for allowing me to take a risk and try a new subject we had never heard of before. I've learned a lot about myself and even ventured further into classical languages such as Pali, in order to explore my Thai-American identity and Buddhist heritage. Thank you to the parents and to the 250+ participants who brought endless energy to our Latin lessons! You allowed me to explore my passion for bringing Latin to a broader audience and become an advocate for Latin within schools in the Pacific Northwest. I hope you all enjoy!

Bene vale,
Taryn Boonpongmanee

ENGLISH

Julia smiled to herself as she looked out of the window. The sky was clear, and the atmosphere was bright. She had not seen such a gorgeous Friday afternoon in a while. Then again, perhaps she felt it was gorgeous because she finally had a day off from soccer practice. As a fourteen-year-old girl, Julia was usually quite busy with her student leader activities, extracurricular club activities, travel, and sports. So, having a rare Friday afternoon all to herself felt like a well-deserved breath of fresh air!

Suddenly, Julia heard the garage door open. It was her mother who had come home early from work. Julia could hear her mom walking around the house, probably changing into her casual clothes. Then, she heard her mom switching on the TV. Julia ran downstairs to greet her mom. Her mom patted the sofa next to her, asking Julia to sit down.

Julia was never one to watch the news, but she liked spending time with her mom. So, she sat down next to her mom and looked at the TV. The news anchor was talking about several wildfires that were spreading through her state and other nearby states on the west coast of America. Three huge wildfires were already happening in Idaho, Oregon, Montana, and Washington. The anchor also remarked that the black smoke would soon be shifting to Julia's town by the weekend.

"I guess we're going to have to prepare for bad weather in the middle of the summer," Julia's mom said with a worried face.

"Yikes," said Julia as she stood up. She let her mom watch the rest of the news and walked toward the pantry, hoping to grab a snack. But she suddenly remembered that it would be better if she could get a head start on her Latin reading assignment, which was given to her by her Latin teacher.

Julia and her mom are watching the news on TV. The anchor is reporting about wildfires.

As a little girl, Julia had become enthralled with Roman and Greek history when she saw the words on buildings in the Latin language. The letters were somewhat unfamiliar to her, so she was curious about what they meant. When she got the chance to take Latin classes in high school, she simply jumped at the chance! She found it to be a rather fascinating field of study.

Her homework assignment for the weekend was to do some reading about Roman gods and goddesses. She grabbed a snack from the pantry and headed upstairs to her bedroom to dive into the reading assignment, excited to learn more about this subject that she had grown to truly love.

Julia sat at her desk by the window and opened her textbook. She really enjoyed reading about the Roman gods and goddesses and their amazing powers. Not long after she began to immerse herself in her reading, Julia heard a loud knock on her window.

"Knock, knock, knock!" She was quite startled by the sound and dropped the cookie she was eating.

"Who's knocking on my window?" she thought as she looked up. But she could not see anything. And then, she heard the knock once again. It sounded like someone invisible was knocking on the window!

"Who's there?" Julia shouted out loud. As if by magic, a flying figure materialized outside her window. It was a man wearing a winged hat while holding a staff with two snakes winding around it! Julia's eyes automatically turned toward her textbook. On the open page, there was an illustration of a man who looked just like the one outside her window. Beneath the picture, the following words were written: "The Roman god Mercury is the god associated with commerce, messages, communication, luck, trickery, and traveling."

"Is that… Mercury?" Julia wondered in astonishment as she looked at the man outside the window.

Julia is sitting at her desk and looking at the window. Mercury, with a friendly smile on his face, is flying outside her window. Julia looks shocked to see him.

She tentatively approached the window and opened it a crack.

"Are you Mercury?" she asked.

"Yes, I am," stated Mercury warmly. "Hello, Julia! It is a pleasure to meet you!"

"How do you know me?" she asked. And then she suddenly took a step back. She wondered whether it was impolite to question a god like that. "Uh… nice staff!" she said, not knowing what else to say.

"Thanks!" Mercury grinned. "Apollo gave it to me as a gift!"

Julia wondered what Mercury was doing outside her window.

As if he could read her thoughts, Mercury answered her unasked question. "Julia, you are cordially invited to the G12 meeting at Mount Olympus," he said, looking her straight in the eye. Julia's eyes grew big in shock and her jaw slacked open in amazement.

"G12?!" she stammered in disbelief. "Are you inviting me to the meeting? ME?!" Julia had learned a little bit about the G12 meeting in her studies. She knew that it was a big meeting of heads of the governments that had a very advanced industrial sector. She also knew that the central bank of this group controlled international finance. "Why me?" Julia could not help but wonder. "Why would I be invited to such a powerful and important meeting?"

Then, she suddenly came to her senses. Mercury was still waiting outside her window, expecting a reply from her. Julia was anxious about taking part in a very serious meeting that discussed world matters, but this was not an opportunity she could let slide. "Cool!" she told Mercury in her most composed voice. "This is an opportunity that I can't pass up! Let's go!"

"Hold on to my hand," said Mercury. "We're going to fly!"

Julia held her breath as she gripped Mercury's hand tightly. In an instant, Mercury and Julia were off! Flying by the power of Mercury's winged helmet while holding onto Mercury's arm on the way to Greece, Julia saw so many fantastic sights. But she couldn't help but notice how tired Mercury looked after they started their journey. His wings sputtered, resulting in a choppy flight, which caused them to bounce up and down suddenly. It made Julia's head start spinning. She could not help but wonder whether Mercury was feeling okay.

"Are you alright?" Julia asked Mercury. "You seem to be getting tired."

"I'm fine," Mercury smiled weakly. "I just drained all my energy. I need to rest often to recharge these days. My power is weaker than it was during the time in ancient Rome. I used to be able to fly from the top of Mount Olympus to the Earth and back quite smoothly, like riding an Airbus A380 or a Boeing 747!"

"What happened to your power?" Julia asked.

Mercury and Julia are flying over a city. Mercury looks a bit tired.

"You will find out in the meeting," Mercury replied. "Meanwhile, don't worry too much. I can still make it with no trouble."After their flight resumed for a few minutes, Mercury seemed to be getting too weary to fly. "We are going to pass the Blue Cloud over the Atlantic Ocean soon," Mercury said, trying to catch his breath.

"Would you like to take a break?" asked Julia. Mercury agreed. Julia was not in a hurry to reach the end of their journey. After all, when would she ever have another opportunity like this to see so much of the world, and from this perspective, in such a short amount of time? She thought to make the best of it. Landing on the Blue Cloud, Mercury found a comfortable resting spot to recharge his energy.

"I may have overestimated myself a bit," he laughed while Julia looked around. "In a few more minutes, can we take another break in Spain?"

"Absolutely!" Julia agreed. A few minutes later, Mercury stood up and said that they could start the journey once again. Still, he looked completely exhausted, could barely walk straight, and looked a bit wobbly. But he insisted on moving forward. And so, both of them took off and landed again in Rome. Julia got a little bit dizzy from going up and down while Mercury's energy ran out.

"I think I should rest a bit more before going up Mount Olympus," he suggested as he collapsed on the ground. Julia could not agree more. She wished that she could carry *him* up Mount Olympus. But alas! She did not have any magical powers. So, all she could do was sit and wait while Mercury lay down and took a long nap. Julia was also nodding off when Mercury suddenly woke up with a jump, startling Julia.

"Come on!" he cried in a hurry. "Let's go!"

And so, Julia held onto Mercury's hand once again. The journey up Mount Olympus was indeed a memorable one.They passed through clouds, leaving the beautiful landscapes of Greece below them. Soon, Mercury and Julia arrived at a golden palace on the top of Mount Olympus. It had magnificent marble pillars and statues of mythical creatures. Julia walked around in awe, gazing left, then right, and turning her head everywhere. She felt completely lost!

"I have never seen anything like this!" she gasped as she looked around in amazement. And then, she caught the sight of the land below them through a wide window.

"Oh my, what a gorgeous view of the earth!" Julia exclaimed.

Mercury led Julia into a beautifully decorated hall where ten seniors in togas and white dresses stood in a circle. They looked just like the ancient gods and goddesses in Julia's Latin book! Julia rubbed her eyes in bewilderment.

"Mercury, I think we are in the wrong room," Julia whispered.

"Julia, you are not in Kansas anymore," said Mercury smiling. "We are in the original G12 meeting. It's the meeting of twelve gods and goddesses."

Julia stood there, shaking nervously. Mercury held Julia's hand and led her as they walked through the circle of gods and goddesses. Julia could feel curious glances falling on her. Mercury introduced Julia to a couple. They looked like they were highly important here. The man wore a golden crown on his head and held a thunderbolt in his hand. The woman wore a goatskin robe.

"Julia, this is Jupiter and Juno, the king and the queen of the Olympian gods and goddesses," Mercury said as he introduced Julia to them.

"Salvete, Mercury and Julia!" said Jupiter. "Welcome to Des Consentes!"

"Hi Julia, it's nice to meet you," said Juno warmly. "I am glad you can attend our meeting."

Julia pinched herself as she stood there speechless.

"Is this real?" she thought. "Where am I?" She was stuttering and sweating when she finally replied, "Nice to meet you!"

Julia is in the meeting of gods and goddesses. Jupiter, Juno, Neptune, Vesta, Ceres, Mars, Vulcan, Minerva, Apollo, and Diana are seated in a circle. Mercury is walking over to his own seat while Julia stares in amazement.

"Let me introduce you to the gods and goddesses of Olympus," said Jupiter. "I'll start with my brother and my sisters. Neptune is my brother. Neptune is the one with the trident. He is the god of the sea and rivers. My sister Ceres is the goddess of agriculture and familial love. My sister Vesta is the goddess of the hearth."

Julia smiled and gulped before replying, "Nice to meet you all!"

"Jupiter and I have many children," said Juno. "Mars is the one with a spear and he is the god of war. Vulcan is the god of fire and metalworks."

"Nice to meet you both, Mars and Vulcan!" Julia said.

Of course, you already met my son, Mercury," said Jupiter. "He is the god of interpretation, communication, and also our messenger. My other children are Minerva, Apollo, Diana, and Venus. Minerva is the goddess of wisdom and Apollo is the god of the Sun. Diana is the goddess of hunting. My other daughter, the beautiful Venus, is the goddess of love and beauty. But she is not here today."

"Oh, how is she doing?" Julia asked.

"Not so good," Jupiter replied with a thoughtful look. "She went shopping in Paris and got locked up at the Louvre Museum."

Julia looked at all the gods and goddesses in wonder. They all had an otherworldly charm to them.

"Have a seat, Julia," Jupiter said as he motioned to a chair near him. Julia did as she was told. She could not help but wonder why she was summoned by these great celestial beings.

"We called for this meeting because we noted that our superpowers are weakening," Jupiter got straight to the point. "We found out that the main cause for this was that fewer people are interested in learning Latin and Greek these days. That's where we need your help, Julia. We receive lots of energy that strengthens our superpower from you because of your intrigue, interest, and passion for Latin and Classics. Every time you study Latin, energy is sent to us."

"But how?" asked Julia. She could not imagine that her interest in Latin had helped these superior beings.

"It's all thanks to astrology!" explained Jupiter. "Our horoscopes show us where you live on our map of the world when you study Latin! We feel a strong passion from you which links to all of us to generate strength and increase our superpower."

"Wow, that's amazing!" Julia exclaimed. "Can you help us spread the word on Latin and Greek studies among young people?" asked Jupiter. "In return, we will grant you a wish!"

Julia thought for a moment. "This is a great idea!" she thought. "I can't believe I am getting a chance to work with the Olympian gods and goddesses." Without further hesitation, she accepted the offer and began thinking of ways to revive Latin and Greek. But what would she wish for? Suddenly, Julia had a thought. "One wish?" she said out loud. "But the Genie gives three wishes…"

"Who is the Genie?" questioned Jupiter, looking rather curious. "I am the king of the gods and goddesses!"

"The Genie is a funny, gigantic spirit in the story Aladdin," Juno reminded Jupiter. Jupiter nodded knowingly.

"Never mind," said Julia with a smile. "One wish is better than none!"

Juno smiled and looked at Julia. "Do you know what your wish is?" she asked.

Julia thought for a moment. There were so many things she could wish for! Suddenly, one thing occurred to her. "There is a wildfire in my hometown," she said. "In the last few years, wildfires lasted the entire summer and we were not able to play outside. The current fire was caused by a lightning bolt in some forest. Could you help me put out the wildfire?"

"Oops!" said Jupiter as he hid his lightning bolt behind his chair. "I think I sneezed and let one of the thunderbolts fall there by accident."

"Ceres, goddess of agriculture, told me that the fire had destroyed a lot of farmlands," Juno noted. "And now that I think about it, Diana, goddess of the hunt, could not hunt because of the smoke from the wildfire. She said animals were going rampant."

"Putting out a fire is a piece of cake!" said Jupiter, waving his hand casually. "Just tell me when and where. I will pour rain into the wildfire for you. Deal?"

"Deal!" Julia exclaimed with a smile. With the agreement in place, Mercury flew Julia back to her room.

"Thank you for agreeing to help us," he said with a smile before flying away.

Julia pondered how she could keep her end of the deal and bring more strength and power to the gods and goddesses. "Perhaps I could spread the message on social media," she thought. "I could make some nice posts about learning Latin… But would that work? I need to make people see how amazing Latin is. Perhaps learning about the Olympian gods and goddesses would do the trick."

She decided that she had to show the world that the Olympian gods and goddesses were relevant in the modern world. Just then, she heard some news on the TV regarding the wildfire.

"I know!" Julia exclaimed. "I can get people interested in Latin by broadcasting Jupiter extinguishing the wildfire! That would give people the chance to see the gods in action!" She thought that it was a genius idea. She could broadcast their actions in English and Latin on TikTok, Instagram, and Twitter! She thought that it would greatly stimulate interest in Latin within the global community.

And so, when Mercury came to visit her the next day, Julia sent a message to Jupiter to ask when he could start the rain.

"I'm afraid I'm a bit busy the next day," replied Jupiter. "But I can make time for you at noon on the day after, during my lunch break."

Julia was not sure whether it would be a good idea to try out her plan to extinguish the fire at noon when the Sun was right overhead, and the temperature was highest. "It'll be okay," she assured herself. "They are gods after all…"

The next day at the appointed time, Julia hiked to the top of a mountain overlooking the wildfire. She was ready to broadcast the event on several social media networks. The weather was very hot and windy as usual. On cue, Jupiter appeared in the sky above the wildfire at noon. The people who were watching Julia's broadcast were quite amazed to see him. The number of views on Julia's broadcast started increasing significantly.

"Here I go!" yelled Jupiter as he got ready to use his powers. He used all of his energy to create a layer of dark rain and clouds above the wildfire. Lightning could be seen rumbling in the sky. The audience was excited to see the clouds and were hopeful about the rain. Finally, the wildfire would be gone! Soon, it started raining heavily. But the Sun still shone brightly in the sky, creating a thermal gradient that made the winds blow strongly. Because of the strong wind, all the rain clouds drifted away!

Julia is standing on top of a mountain, overlooking a burning landscape. She is holding her phone, recording the scene. Jupiter is trying to keep some rain clouds positioned over the wildfire but the wind is pushing them away. Jupiter looks desperate.

"Jupiter, the clouds!" yelled Julia. "They're floating away!" Jupiter tried his best to keep the clouds from floating away, but since his energy was already drained, all he could do was look on. In the end, the rain totally missed the wildfire! The audience was very disappointed. Jupiter could not believe that he could not put out the fire with his mighty power! Feeling bad about what happened, Julia immediately stopped her broadcast.

"I'm sorry," Jupiter told her. "I couldn't keep my end of the promise."

"It's alright," said Julia. "You tried your very best. Perhaps we can try again when you're recharged."

Jupiter thought that it was a great idea. Still, he was feeling quite dejected and frustrated. After going back to Mount Olympus, Jupiter told the other Olympian gods and goddesses about what happened. "I'm afraid that my failed attempt may result in us becoming even weaker," he said. "The people who were watching might have been quite disappointed."

"Don't be upset father," said Minerva, the goddess of wisdom. "We are the Olympians. There is nothing we cannot do if we put our minds to it."

"What are you suggesting?" asked Jupiter.

"I don't think you can do this by yourself," said Minerva. "We should start the mission when the weather is cooler. Possibly in the morning. We could ask Apollo to put away the Sun during the mission. We have to prevent the earth from heating up. We can also ask for help from Neptune, the god of water."

"I can make more water available for evaporation from the Pacific Ocean and the Columbia River," offered Neptune. "As you may know, the Columbia River is the largest river that flows from North America into the Pacific Ocean. With more water evaporating, you would get more rain clouds."

"Fantastic!" said Jupiter, already feeling confident. He asked Mercury to send a message to Julia regarding the new plan which was scheduled for the next morning.

"I think this could really work!" Julia replied with great enthusiasm. She was so excited about the next day that she could hardly sleep.

The next morning, Julia hiked to the top of the mountain and started the broadcast again. This time, her audience was watching with low expectations given their disappointment after the first failed attempt. But they were quite shocked when the Sun was suddenly pulled away from the earth! They wondered whether it was because of a sudden solar eclipse.

Imagine their surprise when they saw Apollo pulling the Sun away! Needless to say, this caused the number of Julia's viewers to skyrocket. When the Sun was pulled away, the surrounding temperature began to drop drastically. The temperature difference caused the winds to shift because of the decreasing thermal gradient. Neptune appeared over the massive Columbia River and flew along the river with his trident in hand. The water began to evaporate and reappeared in the form of huge dark clouds above the wildfire. In the next second, Jupiter appeared in the sky in all his glory, transforming the clouds into massive rain. Julia was in great danger of being rained upon but luckily, Mercury appeared near her, holding a big umbrella.

"It's working!" Julia cried happily as the heavy rain poured all around them.

"Yes, it is," Mercury smiled. "Do you think we caused enough of a stir?"

"Oh, I think you did!" said Julia, looking at her social media broadcast. It already had over a million views! The gods celebrated their successful mission while the rain completely extinguished the raging wildfire.

"We did it!" exclaimed Jupiter as he did a fancy touchdown move he had seen on Tik Tok. Then, he winked at Julia before disappearing. Apollo dragged the Sun back into its rightful position. Neptune did not have to do anything since all the evaporated water had already landed back on the ground in the form of rain. Julia smiled happily as she saw her audience cheering for Jupiter and the other gods. Some of the members of the audience were even messaging in Latin thanking the gods for their assistance. The Latin word "gratias" was probably the most commonly used word on the internet that day. Needless to say, this boosted the power of the gods significantly. Within the next few days, a popular GIF appeared to promote Latin classes all over the world. The GIF included a picture of Jupiter's touchdown move! And then, texting in Latin became the next coolest thing.

Everyone wanted to appear cool among their colleagues and started learning Latin. Even people who had no idea about what Latin was started looking it up and developed an interest in learning it. They wanted to learn more about the amazing Olympian gods and goddesses who had put out the massive fire that threatened to destroy everything. Some Latin classes even had a waitlist thanks to all the people wanting to sign up. Julia's Latin teacher was also quite surprised by the sudden increase in the number of students in her class. But she wasn't going to complain about it!

At Mount Olympus, the gods and goddesses were watching everything. They were quite happy with how things had worked out. They were also very impressed with how Julia managed to solve their problem and her problem in one go. With every student who signed up for learning Latin, the gods and goddesses could feel their strength getting stronger and stronger! Once again, they summoned Julia to Mount Olympus to thank her for what she had done for them. Mercury, in his usual enthusiasm and cheerful nature, came to pick up Julia. This time, when she held his hand, Julia could almost feel the divine power emanating from him. He looked much stronger and happier.

"Hold on to your shoes, Julia!" he laughed as he took to the sky. "This journey is going to be much faster than our last one. And it's all thanks to you!" It didn't take them long to arrive at the top of Mount Olympus. Mercury did not have to stop on the way to rest even once!

After entering the great hall of the gods, Julia was welcomed warmly by the gods and goddesses. They presented her with an olive crown, a kotinos, much like the ones given at the ancient Olympic Games.

"This kotinos holds magical power," said Jupiter. "Next time you want to visit us, simply put on the kotinos and think of us. It will bring you here. We're forever grateful for what you did for us. Consider this kotinos as a small token of our gratitude."

"You're always welcome among us," smiled Juno.

"Thank you!" said Julia as she accepted the kotinos. When Juno put it on Julia's head, all the gods and goddesses applauded and cheered.

LATIN

Iulia, per fenestram spectans, surrisit. Caelum apertum erat et aer clarus erat. Tam pulchrem diem Veneris dum non viderat. Tamen fortasse sensit splendidam esse quod dies sine exercitatione erat. Ut puella cottidianus quattuordecim annorum, Iulia saepe discipula cum principi actionibus, ludis, itineribus, et iocis occupata erat. Sic raram diem Veneris pro se reliquam habere eam animavit.

Subito, Iulia portam apertam esse audivit. Eius mater mane e labore reveniebat. Iulia matrem ambulare per villam audivit. Probabiliter se vestiebat. Iulia ad matrem cucurrit ut eam salutaret. Mater lectum prope eam ostendit, orans ut Iulia sedeat.

Iuliae numquam curae nuntia erant, sed esse cum matre amabat. Sic prope matrem sedit et nuntia audivit. Nuntius de multibus incendiis augentibus per provincas Iuliae et per alias provincias in litore occidentale Americae nuntiabat. Tria incendia ingentia erant in Idahone, in Oregone, in Montana, et in Washingtone. Nuntius dixit tenebrosum fumum mox venturum esse ad urbem Iuliae.

„Necesse erit parare malae tempestati in media aestate," Iuliae mater inquit, cum anxiosa facie.

„Heu!" Iulia adsurgens dixit. Matrem reliquit in lecto et ad carnarium iit ut ederet. Sed subito meminit legendum, quod Latinae magistra ei dedit, melius esse.

Iulia et mater nuntia spectant. Nuntius de incindibus nuntiabat.

Iulia amabat Romae et Graeciae historiam postquam, ut puella, verba scripta in lingua Latina in Senatus muris videt. Litterae incognitae sibi erant, itaque curiosa erat quod significarent. Cum potuisset Latinam studere in schola, progressa est. Lingua Latina eam animavit.

Debebat legere de deis et deabus Romanis. Ferens, in cubiculum iit ut legeret, cupiens discere de lingua quam amabat.

Iulia in mensa, quam iuxta fenestram erat, sedit et librum aperuit. De Romanis et Graecis deis deabusque et suis viribus mirabilibus legere amabat. Mox postquam legere incepit, Iulia pulsum magnum fenestram offendere audivit.

„Pulsus, pulsus, pulsus!" Territa est sono et crustulum demisit.

Occuli tollens, mirata est, „Qui meam fenestram pulsavit?" Sed nihil videt. Tum, pulsum alium audivit. aliquis invisibilis fenestram offendere visus est.

„Qui est?" Iulia clamavit.

Sicut magice, volans figura extra fenestram apparuit. Vir erat qui alatum petasum gerebat et baculum duobus serpentibus circumcinctum portabat. Iuliae oculi ad librum verterunt. In pagina erat vir similis figurae quae erat extra fenestram. Sub pictura, heac verba erant: Mercurius, Deus Romanus communicationis, nuntiorum, itinerum, commerciorum, fortunae, dolorum erat.

„Mercurius …est?" Iulia mirata est, spectans virum extra fenestram.

Iulia sedet in pulpito et fenestram spectat. Mercurius extra fenestram volat, amice surridens. Iulia vexamine eum spectat.

Ea caute fenestrae appropinquavit et minime aperuit. „Mercurius es?" rogavit.

„Ita vero, sum!" Mercurius inquit. „Salve, Iulia, gaudeo te congredi. "

„Quomodo me cognoscis?" rogavit. Subito recessit et meditata est num importunus esset ita loqui cum deo.

„Pulcherrimum baculum habes!" inquit, non sciens quod esset dicendum.

„Gratias tibi ago!" Mercurius exclamavit. „Apollo donum mihi dedit."

Iulia mirabatur cur Mercurius extra fenestram esset.

Mercurius respondit ut scivit quod putaret.
„Iulia, ad G12 congressum, qui erit in monte Olympi, amice te invito," inquit, oculos spectans.

Iuliae oculi stupore aperti erant et os laxata est.

„G12?!" Admiratione dixit. „Tu me invitas ad congressum? ME?!"

Iulia de G12 congressu paulum studuit. Magnae industriae maximum congressum esse, eius industriam optimam esse, et argentariam centicam congressus internationalem pecuniam regere cognovit. „Cur me?" Iulia se rogavit. „Cur sum invitata ad congressum tam fortem gravemque?"

Tum subito meminit Mercurium deforis manens, responsum expectantem. Iulia anxiosa erat quod congressus tam graviosus erat, ubi de rebus totius orbis conlocuti sunt, sed optimam oportunitatem non potuit perdere. „Optime!" inquit Mercurio aequanima voce. „Oportunitatem non possum perdere! venimus!"

„Tene meam manum," Mercurius inquit. „Volabimus!"

Iulia spiritum retinuit, haerens Mercurii manui. Mercurius et Iulia statim discesserunt. Viribus Mercurii aliferae cornus ad Graeciam volans haerensque Mercurii brachio, Iulia fabulosas conspectiones vidit. Sed mox vidit Mercurium fessum esse. Alae eius, subito dissultantes, tremuerunt, et volatus interruptus est. Iulia cogitavit num Mercurius bene sentiret.

„Es bene?" Iulia Mercurio rogavit. „Fessus esse videris."

„Bene sum." Mercurius infirme risit. „Vis siccatur. Debeo requiescere. Mei vires pauliores sunt quam in tempore antiquae Romae. Volare poteram de Olympi ad terram rursumque mollius, sicut in Airbus A380 aut Boeing 747 portabamur."

„Quid accidit?" Iulia interrogavit.

Mercurius Iuliaque super urbem volant. Mercurius fessus videtur.

„In consilio disces," Mercurius respondit. „Noli se sollicitare ante eum, faciliter succedere possum."

Resumpto volatu brevi tempore, Mercurius visus est tam fessus ut non volare posset. „Mox perveniemus Blavium Nubem, qui est super Atlanticum Oceanum," Mercurius inquit, exanimis.

„Vis consistere?" Iulia rogavit.

„Certe!" Mercurius respondit. Iulia non festinabat iter perficere. Ubi tam fortunata erit ut videre mundum, e tale loco, et tam brevi tempore posset? Iter delectavit. Decurrens in Blavium Nubem, Mercurius, locum invenit ut requiesceret et vim recuperaret.

„Fortasse sensi me posse facere magis quam potui!" risit, Iulia spectanti. „Mox requiescere poterimus in Hispania?"

„Certe!" Iulia constavit. Postmodum, Mercurius surrexit et dixit itinerem incipere se posse. Tamen fessus erat, ambulare paene poterat, et instabile erat. Sed progredi voluit. Itaque, volabant et in Roma constiterunt. Iulia calligatur volatu et Mercurius effetus erat.

„Requiescendum mihi esse reor antequam ascendere montem Olympum," dixit, ad terram decidens. Iulia constitit. Utinam eum portare ea posset ad montem Olympus. Heu! Magicas vires non habuit. Itaque, non potuit facere magis quam sedere et manere, Mercurio reclinante et longe dormiente. Iulia incipiente dormire, Mercurius tam subito saluit quam Iulia consternata est.

„Veni!" celeriter inquit. „Venimus!"

Igitur, Iulia Mercurii manum iterum tenuit. Subire montem Olympus memorabile fuit. Nubes pervenerunt, pulcherrimam terram Graeciae relinquentes. Mox, Mercurius et Iulia ad auream aulam montis Olympi advenerunt. Magnificae marmoreae columnae et fabulosae creaturae erant. Iulia mirata est, dextrorsum sinistrorsumque spectans, ubiquaque caput. Perdita erat!

„Numquam talem vidi!" clamavit, circumspectans admiratione. Tum, terram sub eis per fenestram conspexit.

„Ecce, optima terra!" Iulia inquit.

Mercurius Iuliam in pulcherrime aulam duxit ubi decem senes togati et gerentes habitus candidos in corona sedebant. Imitabantur deis deabusque qui erant in Latinae libro Iuliae! Iulia perplexa erat, oculos tergens.

„Mercurie, credo nos in inuria esse," Iulia mussavit.

„Iulia, non iam in Kansase es," inquit Mercurius ridens. „In vero G12 consilo sumus. Duodecim deorum dearumque consilium est."

Iulia trepide tremebat. Mercurius eius manum tenebat, ducens eam per deos deasque. Iulia omnium adspectus sensit. Mercurius Iuliam coniugio introduxit. Gravissimi visi sunt. Vir auream coronam super caput portavit et in manu dextro fulmen tenuit. Femina togam caprigenam portavit.

„Iulia, Jupiter et Juno sunt, rex reginaque Olympianorum deorum dearumque," Mercurius inquit, Iulia introducta.

„Salvete, Mercurie et Iulia!" inquit Jupiter. „Hic Des Constentes est!"

„Salve, Iulia, gaudeo te congredi," Iuno amice inquit. „Gaudeo quod ad nostrum consilium venis."

„Verum est?" Iulia cogitavit. „Ubi sum?" Balbutiens et sudans respondit. „Gaudeo te congredi!"

Iulia in consilio deorum dearumque est. Jupiter, Iuno, Neptunus, Vesta, Ceres, Mars, Vulcanus, Minerva, Apollo et Diana sedebant in corona. Mercurius suam sedem advenit dum Iulia miratur.

„Te introducam deis deabusque Olympi," Iupiter inquit. „Primo, mei frater et sorores. Neptunus mei fratres est. Neptunus tridentem tenet. Is deus maris et fluminum est. Mea soror Ceres agriculturae familiaeque dea est. Mea soror Vesta foci dea est. "

Iulia surrisit antequam respondit, „Gaudeo vos congredi."

„Ego et Iupiter multos pulchros liberos habemus," Iuno inquit. „Mars hastam tenet deus belli est. Vulcanus ignis et ferrarii laboris deus est."

„Gaudeo vos congredi, Mars et Vulcane!" Iulia inquit.

„Quippe, iam cum meo filio congressus es, Mercurio" inquit Jupiter. „Is interpretationis, communicationis deus est et noster nuntius. Mei alteri filii et filiae Minerva, Apollo, Diana, et Venus sunt. Minerva dea sapientiae et Apollo deus Solis est.

Diana dea venationis est. Mea altera filia, pulchra Venus, amoris et pulchritudinis dea est. Non est hic hodie."

„Bene est?" Iulia rogavit.

„Bene non est," Iuputer respondit cogitabundus. „In Parisibus ea obsonavit et in Louvri Museo inclusa erat."

Iulia mirata deos deasque spectavit. Omnes incredibile magicos habebant.

„Sede, Iulia," Jupiter dixit, sedem prope se ostendens. Iulia fecit hoc. Iulia deliberavit cur a deis vocata esset.

„Consilium convocavimus quod nostri vires infirmiores fiunt," Iupiter breviter dixit. „Quod hodie pauciores linguas Latinae et Graeciae student. Itaque opus est nobis tuo auxilio, Iulia. Omnes potestatem a te accepimus propter tuam amorem Latinae. Quotiens Latinae studes, totiens vires accipimus."

„Quomodo?" Iulia rogavit. Non putavit suum studium deos iuvare posse.

„Propter astrologiam est!" Jupiter explicavit. „Nostri horoscopi ardent et nobis ostendent ubi in mundo tu Latinam studes! Tuas vires fortes sentimus, quae nos iuvant fortiores fieri."

„O! Mirabilis est!" Iulia exclamavit. „Potes nos iuvare pandere linguas Latinae et Graeciae ad iuvenes?" Iupiter rogavit, „Tibi rursum unum voluntatem dabimus"

Iulia paulisper cogitavit. „Optimum decretum est!" credidit. „Non credo me posse cum deis deabusque Olympi laborare." Sine mora oportunitatem accepit et quomodo posset recuperare Latinam et Graecam cogitavit. Sed quod cupivit? Subito, Iulia sententiam habuit. „Unum voluntatem?" clamavit. „Spiritus tria voluntates dat…"

„Qui est spiritus?" Iupiter curiosus rogavit. „Ego rex deorum dearumque sum!"

„Spiritus iocosus ingensque in Aladdini fabula est." Iuno Iovem admonuit. Iupiter scienter adnuit.

„A bene," Iulia ridens inquit. „Unum voluntatem melius quam nullum est!"

Iuno surrisit et Iuliam spectavit. „Tu scis quid cupias?" rogavit.

Iulia paulisper deliberavit. Cupivit multas res. Subito, de una re cogitavit. „Incendium est in mea urbe," inquit. „Incendia tota aestate erant et ludere deforis non potuimus. Causa huius incendi fulgor in aliquibus silvis erat. Potes me iuvare stinguere incendia?"

„Eheu!" inquit Iupiter, fulgorem post sedem ponens. „Reor me sternuisse et errore unum emittere."

„Ceres, agriculturae dea, dixit incendium multos agros conrumpere," Iuno annotavit, „et non censeo Dianam, venationis deam, venari potuisse, fumi causa. Dixit animalia feroces esse."

„Incendia stinguere facile est!" Iupiter locutus est, manum constanter concutens. „Dic mihi ubi et quando sint! Impluam in incendia pro te. Concurrimus?"

„Concurrimus!" Iulia clamavit, ridens.

Concordia facta, Mercurius volavit cum Iulia in cubiculum.

„Gratias tibi ago quod nos iuvas!" is dixit antequam discessit.

Iulia meditata est quomodo concordiam, honorem, et fortiores deos faciat. „Fortasse ubiquaque nuntiare possum," cogitavit. „Pulchra carmina de Latina scribam …sed utilis erit? Omnes debent prendere quam Latina mirifica est. Fortasse de Olympi deis deabusque discere utile erit."

Dignavit se debere ostendere hominibus deos deasque etiam hodie graves esse. Tum nuntia de incendiis audit.

„Scio!" Iulia clamavit. „Possum Iovem desseminare incendia stinguentem! Omnes acta deorum videre poterunt!" Dignavit eam cogitationem optimam esse. Acta deorum transmittentur, Latine atque Anglice, per Tiktok, Instagram, Twitterque. Amorem Latinae discipulae in tota orbe terrarum hoc augere cogitavit.

Cum Mercurius cras eam visitaret, Iulia nuntium misit Iovi, rogans quando impluaret.

„Incommode cras occupatus ero," respondit Jupiter. „Sed potero post meridiem, proxima die, ubi edam."

Iulia dubitabat num prudens esset meridie incendia stinguere conari ubi sol altissimus erat et maximus caldor erat. „Bene erit!" dixit sibi. „Quod dei sunt…."

Proxima die, stato tempo, Iulia ad summum montis despectens incendia subiit. Preparata erat undique disseminare. Tempus calidus et ventosus erat. Signe dato, Iupiter in caelo apparuit super incendia meridie. Omnes qui spectabant cum eum vidissent mirati sunt. Numerus spectatorum crevit.

„Venimus!" Iupiter clamavit, parans viribus uti.

Totis viribus usus est ut nubes caecos super incendia faceret. Multitudo hominum excita est nubes videns, et pluviam speraverunt. Tandem, incendium finitum erit! Mox impluere incepit. Sed sol etiam ita clare lucebat in caelo ut ventus fortiter perflaveret. Venti pluviosas nubes pepullerunt.

Iulia in summo monte sedet, ardentem terram adspectans. Iupiter super incendia nubes pluvias tenere conatur, sed ventus pepulit. Iupiter desperat.

„Iupiter, nubes!" Iulia clamavit. „Discedent!"

Iupiter conatus est nubes tenere, sed viribus depletis, miser spectavit… tandem, pluvia defuit. Turba desituta est. Iupiter non credidit se incedium stinguere non potuisse viribus suis. Triste, Iulia nuntiare finit.

„Paeniteo," Iupiter ei dixit, „facere quod dixi non potuit."

„Bene est," Iulia dixit. „Fortiter conatus es. Fortasse conabimur ubi eris fortior."

Iupiter eum bonum decretum dignitavit. etiam, iratus et abiectus erat. Postquam revenit ad montem Olympi, Iupiter dixit deis deabusque totam rem. „Timeo ne conatus meus nos faciat infirmiores," dixit. „Fortasse spectatores destituti sunt."

„Noli esse triste, Pater," inquit Minerva, sapientiae dea. „Sumus dei Olympi. Omnia potemus facere si meditamur."

„Quid suades?" Iupiter rogavit.

„Non credo te solum posse hoc facere." Minerva dixit. „Debemus incipere ubi tempus frigidior est, fortasse ante meridiem. Possumus Apolloni persuadere ut solem demoveret nobis loborantibus. Impedire debemus terram quominus calefaciat. Precari ut Neptunus, deus aquae, nos iuvat possumus."

„Possum vobis dare magis aquae pro evaporatione, e Pacifici Oceano et Columbiae Flumine," obtulit Neptunus. „Fortasse scis flumen Columbiae Flumen maximum esse quod fluet de America Boreae ad Pacifici Oceanum. Quanta aqua, tanta pluvia."

„Optime!" inquit Jupiter, confidens. Mercurium oravit ut novum consilium proximae diei Iuliae nuntiet.

„Credo nos victuros esse!" Iulia acriter respondit. Tam incitata erat de proxima die ut non posset dormire.

Cras, Iulia ad summum montem subiit et nuntiare iterum incepit. Nunc, homines depressis expectationibus spectabant causa primae frustrationis. Ceterum, mirati sunt ubi sol detortus est subito! Viderunt Apollinem solem trahentem de terra! Num solis abruptus defectus esset meditati sunt. Consternati sunt ubi Apollo solem detraxit! Quippe, numerus spectatorum crevit.

Sole detorto, caldor celeriter decidere incepit. Mutationis tempi causa et declivitate decrescente, venti mutati sunt. Neptunus visus est, super flumen ingens Columbiae volans, vibrans tridentem. Aquae incepit tabescere et ingentes nubes nigras super incendium factae sunt. Statim Iupiter in caelo apparuit in tota gloria, et viribus nubes pluvia factae sunt. Iulia paene diluta est, sed feliciter Mercurius apparuit prope eam, magnam umbrellam tenens.

„Vincemus!" Iulia feliciter clamavit dum graviter pluvit ubiquaque.

„Ita vero" Mercurius surrisit. „Credis satis nos fecisse?"

„Ita vero!" Iulia inquit. Iam millia hominum spectaverant. Dei celebraverunt eorum consilium dum pluvia incendia ferocia stinguit.

„Vicimus!" Jupiter clamavit, decurrens agens ballandum motum, ut in Tiktok viderat. Tunc Iupiter adnictavit Iuliae antequam disparuit. Apollo solem in positionem alteram retraxit. Neptunus nihil facit quod exhalata aqua iam ut pluvia in terra erat. Iulia feliciter risit dum turba clamat pro Iove et deis. Aliqui in Latina scribebant, cum gratitudine pro deis. Verbo „gratias!" saepissime illa die usi sunt. Quippe, deorum vires maxime aucti sunt. Paucis diebus, famosa imago Latinae ubiquaque apparuit, lingam colens. Imago Iovis eius ballandum motum erat.

Tunc, Latine loqui populare factus est. Omnes qui pulchri esse volunt, Latinam studere coeperunt. Homines qui Latinam non cognoverunt, discere coeperunt, et eam amaverunt.

Multa discere voluerunt de Olympi deis deabusque qui incendia corrumpserunt quae omnia minata sunt. Aliqui ludi Latinae tam populares erant quam studiosi manere deberent. Magistra Iuliae mirata est turbam discipulorum. Sed non irata est. de monte Olympi dei deaeque omnia spectabant. Felices erunt quod res solverunt. Mirati sunt Iuliam suam rem et eorum rem resolventem. Quotiescumque studiosi Latinam discere inceperunt, vires deorum dearumque fortiores factae sunt.

Iterum Iuliam accerserunt ad montem Olympo ut ei gratias darent convocaverunt. Mercurius, benevolens et laetus natura, ad Iuliam iuvandam venit. Dum manum tenet, Iulia vires de hoc emanantes paene sensit. Magis fortior et laetior erat.

„Tene sotulares, Iulia!" risit ascendens ad caelum. „Iter multo celerius quam ultimum, causa tui!" Celeriter pervenerunt ad summum montem Olympi. Mercurius requiescere numquam debuit.

Postquam intravit magnam aulam deorum, Iulia accepta est deis deabusque. Ei donum dederunt, olivae coronam, kotinos, sicut in Olympiae Ludis.

„Kotinos magicam potestatem," inquit Jupiter. „Si vis venire ad nos, kotinos indue et puta de nobis. Eris hic. Semper gratias tibi agemus pro actis tuis. Kotinos signum gratitudinis est."

„Tu semper inter nos accepta eris," Juno surrisit.
„Gratias tibi ago!" inquit Iulia, kotinos accipiens. Iunone induente kotinos in caput Iuliae, omnes dei deaeque adplauserunt et clamaverunt.

Glossary

a, ab = by (+abl)

abicio, abicere, abieci, abiectus = throw, cast aside

abiectus, a, um = dejected

abrumpo, abrumpere, abrupi, abruptus = break off

accideo, cidere, cidi = happen

accipio, cipere, cepi, ceptum = receive

acriter = fiercly

actio, onis (f) = activity

ad = to, towards (+acc)

admiratio, onis (f) = admiration, wonder

admoneo, admonere, admonui, admonitus = remind

adnicto, adnictare, adnictavi, adnicatus = wink

adplaudo, adplaudere, adplausi, adplasus = applaud

adspicio, adspicere, adspexi, adspectus = observe, see

adsurgo, adsurgere, adsurrexi, adsurrectus = rise up

advenio, advenire, adveni, adventus = arrive

aedificium, i (n) = building

aer, aeris (m) = atmopshere, air

aestas, atis (f) = summer

ager, agri (m) = field

ago, agere, egi, actus = do, drive, act

agricultura, ae (f) = agriculture

ala, ae (f) = wing

Aladdini = Aladdin

alatus, a, um = winged

aliferus, a, um = winged

aliquis, quae, quod = some, any

alius, alia, aliud = other, another

alter, altera, alterum = other

altus, a, um = tall

ambulo, are, avi, atus = walk

America Boreae = North America

America, ae (f) = America

amicale(friendly, cordially) = warmly

amice = cordially

amo, are, avi, atus = love

amor, oris (m) = love

Anglice = English

animal, alis (n) = animal

animo, are, avi, atus = energize, enliven

annoto, are, avi, atus = note

annuo, annuere, annui, annutus = nod

annus, i (m) = year

ante = before (+acc)

antequam = before

anxiosus, a, um = anxious

aperio, aperire, aperui, apertus = open, uncover

Apollo = Apollo (in Greek = Apollo)

appareo, ere, ui = appear

appropinquo, are, avi, atus = approach

aqua, ae (f) = water

ardeo, ardere, arsi, arsus = sparkle, spotlight

argentarius, a, um = of money

asperiter = drastically

astrologia, ae (f) = astrology

Atlanticum Oceanum = the Atlantic Ocean

audio, ire, ivi/ii, itus = hear

augeo, augere, auxi, auctus = increase, spread

aula, ae (f) = courtyard, hall

aureus, a, um = golden

aut = or

auxilium, i (n) = assistance, support

baculum, i (n) = staff

balbus, a, um, as an adjective = stuttering

balbutio, - , - , ire = stutter, stammer

ballo, are, avi, atus = dance

bellum, i (n) = war

bene = well

benevolens, benevolentis = friendly, kind

Blavium Nubes = the Blue Cloud (inspired by Cloud Blue, a hotel in Mykonos, Greece)

bracchium, i (n) = arm

brevis, e = short

caecus, a, um = dark

caelum, i (n) = sky, heavens

caldor, oris (m) = warmth, heat

calefacio, calefacere, calefeci, calefactus = make warm

calidus, a, um = warm

calligo, are, avi, atus = make dizzy

candidus, a, um = clear, white, bright

capio, capere, cepi, captus = take, seize, capture

caprigenam togam = goatskin

caput, capitis (n) = head

carmen, inis (n) = song

carnarium, ii (n) = pantry

causa, ae (f) = cause

caute (meaning more carefully) = tentatively

celebro, are, avi, atus = celebrate

celeriter = quickly

censeo, consere, censui, census = assess, determine

centrum, i (n) = center

Ceres = Ceres (in Greek = Demeter)
cerno, cernere, crevi, cretus = separate
certe = certainly
ceterus, a, um = the other
circumcinctura = encircle
circumspecto, are, avi, atus = look around
clamo, are, avi, atus = call out
clarus, a, um = bright
cogitabundus, a, um = thinking
cogito, are, avi, atus = ponder, think
cognosco, gnoscere, gnovi, gnitus = learn,
understand
collossaeus, a, um = gigantic
Columbiae Flumen = the Columbia River
columna, ae (f) = column, pillar
commercium = trade, traffic, commerce
commiscuissime = commonly
communicatio, onis (f) = communication,
messaging
concordia, ae (f) = harmony, agreeing
together
concurro, concurrere, concucurri,
concursus = agree
concutio, concutere, concussi, concussum
= wave
confido, confidere, confisus = confident,
trust (+dat)
congredior, congredi, congressus sum =
meet, come
congressus, us (m) = meeting
coniugo, are, avi, atus = join
conor, conari, conatus sum = try, attempt
consilium, i (n) = council; plan
consisto, consistere, constiti, constitus =
take a break
conspectio, conspectionis (f) – look, sight
conspicio, conspicere, conspexi,
conspectus = observe, perceive
(attentively)
constanter = resolutely
consterno, are, avi, atus = terrify, alarm
consto, constare, constiti = agree
convoco, are, avi, atus = assemble
corona, ae (f) = wreath, crown
corrumpo, rumpere, rupi, ruptus = break
up, destroy, ruin
corus, us (n) = helmet
cottidianus, a, um = daily
cras – tomorrow, the next day
creatura, ae (f) = creature
credo, credere, credidi, creditus = believe
crustulum, i (n) = cookie
cubiculum, ii (n) = bedroom
cum = with (+abl); when, since (conj +
subjunctive)
cupio, ere, ivi, itus = desire

cur = why
cura, ae (f) = care, concern
curiosus, a, um = curious
curro, currere, cucurri, cursus = run
de = about (+abl)
(de/re)traho, trahere, traxi, tractus = drag
dea, ae (f) = goddess
debeo, debere, debui, debitus = ought to,
should
decem = ten
decerno, cernere, crevi, cretum = decide,
determine
decido, decidere, decidi, decisus =
collapse
declivitas, atis (f) = slope
decresco, decrescere, decrevi, decretus =
decrease
decurro, decurrere, decucurri, decursus =
moving down
deficio, deficere, defeci, defectus = fall
away
deforis = outside
delecto, are, avi, atus = delight, fascinate
delibero, are, avi, atus = consider,
deliberate
demitto, ere, demisi, demissus = drop
demoveo, demovere, demovi, demotus =
move, put away
depleo, deplere, deplevi, depletus – drain
deprimo, deprimere, depressi, depressus =
push down
despecto, are, avi, atus = look down
despero, are, avi, atus = to be hopeless,
give up
destituo, destituere, destitui, destitus = let
down
detorqueo, detorquere, detorsi, detortus =
turn away
deus, i (m) = god
dexter, dextra, dextrum = right
Diana = Diana (in Greek = Artemis)
dico, dicere, dixi, dictus = say
dies Veneris = Friday, day of Venus
dies, diei (m/f) = day
differo, differre, distuli, dilatus =
disperse, scatter
digno, are, avi, atus = consider
diluo, diluere, dilui, dilutus = drench
discedo, ere, cessi, cessus = depart
discipula, ae (f) = student (female)
discipulus, i (m) = student (male)
disco, discere, didici = learn
dissemino, desseminare, desseminavi,
desseminatus = broadcast
do, dare, dedi, datus = give
dolus, i (m) = deceit

donum, i (n) = gift

dormio, dormire, dormivi, dormitus = sleep

dubito, are, avi, atus = uncertain, waver

duco, ducere, duxi, ductus = lead

dum = while

duo, duae, duo = two

duodecim = twelve

ecce = look! see! behold!

edo, edere, edi, esus = eat

effetus, a, um = dizzy, worn out

effligo, ere, efflexi, efflectus = destroy

ego, mei, mihi, me = I, me

emano, are, avi, atus = emanating

emitto, emittere, emisi, emissus = send out

energia, ae (f) = energy

eo, ire, ivi (ii), itus = go

error, oris (m) = error, accident, mistake

et = and; et... et = both... and

etiam = even, also

evaporatio, onis (f) = evaporation

ex, e = out of, from (+abl)

exanimis, e = exhausted, lifeless

excito, are, avi, atus = rouse, excite

exclamo, are, avi, atus = exclaim

exercitatio, onis (f) = practice

explico, are, avi, atus = explain

exspecto, are, avi, atus = expect, wait

exstinguo, ere, exstinxi, exstinctus = extinguish, put out

extra = on the outside

fabula, ae (f) = story

fabulosus, a, um = mythical

facies, faciei (f) = face

facilis, e = easily

facio, facere, feci, factus = do, make

familia, ae (f) = family

famosus, a, um = famous

feliciter = luckily

femina, ae (f) = woman

fenestra, ae (f) = window

fero, ferre, tuli, latus = bear, carry

ferox, ocis = wild

ferrarius, a, um = blacksmiths

fessus, a, um = tired

festino, are, avi, atus = hasten

figura, ae (f) = form, figure

filia, ae (f) = daughter

filius, i (m) = son

finio, finire, finivi, finitus = define

flamma, ae (f)= fire

flumen, inis (n) = river

fluo, fluere, fluxi, fluctus = fall, flow

focus, i (m) = hearth

fortasse = perhaps

fortis, e = powerful; such a powerful...; strong

fortissimus, a, um = most powerful

fortuna, ae, (f) = fortune

fortuno, are, avi, atus = make fortunate or happy

frater, fratris (m) = brother

frigidus, a, um = cold

frustratio, onis (f) = disappointment

frustratus, a, um = frustrated

fulgor, oris (m) = lightning

fulmen, inis (n) ; pessulus, i (m) = thunderbolt

fumus, i (m) = smoke, fume

gaudeo, gaudere, gavisus sum = rejoice

gero, gerere, gessi, gestum = wear

gloria, ae (f) = glory

Graecia, ae (f) = Greece

gratias tibi ego = I thank you

gratitudo, gratitudinis (f) = gratitude

gravis, e = serious

graviter = heavily

gymnasium, ii (n) –type of school = elementary (school)

habeo, habere, habui, habitus = have

haereo, haerere, haesi, haesum = cling to

hasta, ae (f) = spear

heu = oh! alas!

hic, haec, hoc = this, these

Hispania, ae (f) = Spain

historia, ae (f) = history

hodie = today

homo, hominis (m) = human

honor, oris (m) = honor

horoscopus, i (m) = horoscope

iam = now, already

Idahone = Idaho

idea, ae (f) = idea

igitur = therefore

ignis, is (m) = fire

ille, illa, illud = that, those

imaginor, ari, imaginatus sum = imagine

imago, inis (f) = image

imitor, imitari, imitatus sum = imitate, copy, follow

impluo, impluere, implui, implutus = rain

importunus, a, um = unfit, impolite

in = in, on (+abl), into, onto (+acc)

incendium, ii (n) = wildfire, fire

incipio, incipere, incepi, inceptus = begin

incito, are, avi, atus = set in motion

includo, includere, inclusi, inclusum = lock, shut

incognitus, a, um = unfamiliar

incommode = unsuitable, troublesome

incredibilis, e = extraordinary, incredible

induo, induere, indui, indutus = put on
industria, ae (f) (meaning more of dilligence) = industrial sector
infere = beneath
infirmus, a, um = weak
ingens, ingentis = huge, enormous, vast
inquam, inquis, inquit, inquiunt = say (direct speech)
instabilis, e = wobbly
inter = between
internationalis, e = international
interpretatio, onis (f) = interpretation
interrumpo, interrumpere, interrupi, interruptus = interrupt
interruptus, a, um = choppy
intro, are, avi, atus = enter
introduco, introducere, duxi, ductus = lead, bring into a place, introduce
inuria, ae (f) = wrong (wrong place, used substantively)
invenio, invenire, inveni, inventus = find
invisibil, is = invisible
invitatus, a, um = summoned
invito, are, avi, atus = invite
iocosus, a, um = funny
iocus, i (m) = (sports) game
is, ea, id = that (he/she/it)
ita = thus, so
ita vero = truly so (yes)
itaque = and so, therefore
iter, itineris (n) = journey, travel
iterum = again
Iulia, ae (f) = Julia
Iuno = Juno (in Greek = Hera)
Iupiter = Jupiter (in Greek = Zeus)
iuvenis, is (m) = youth, young people
iuvo, are, avi, atus = help
Kansase = Kansas
kotinos (Greek word) = wreath given to winner of the ancient Olympics
labor, oris (m) = work
laboro, are, avi, atus = work
laetus, a, um = happy
Latina, ae (f) = Latin
laxatus, a, um (as an adjective) = slacked
laxo, are, avi, atus = open, strecth
lectus, i (m) = couch
lego, legere, legi, lectus = read
liber, i (m) = textbook
libera, libera, liberum = free; (freeborn) children
lingua, ae (f) = language
littera, ae (f) = letter, alphabet
litus, litoris (n) = coast, shore
locus, i (m) = place
longe = far, far off

loquor, loqui, locutus sum = speak, talk
Louvri Museo = the Louvre Museum
luceo, lucere, luxi = be clear
ludo, ludere, lusi, lusus = play
ludus, i (m) = activity (extracurricular activity)
magice = magic, sorcery
magicus, a, um = magical
magis = significantly (much more)
magistra, ae (f) = teacher
magnificus, a, um = noble, distinguished
magnus, a, um = massive, large, great
malus, a, um = bad
mane = early
maneo, manere, mansi, mansus = remain
manus, us (f) = hand
mare, is (n) = sea
marmoreus, a,um = made of marble
Mars = Mars (in Greek = Ares)
mater, matris (f) = mother
maximus, a, um = biggest
meditor, meditari, meditatus = consider
medius, a, um = middle
melius = better
memini, isse, meministi = remember
memorabilis, e = memorable
mensa, ae (f) = table
Mercurius, i (m) = Mercury (in Greek = Hermes)
meridiem = noon
meus, a, um = my
mificus, a, um = admirable, wonderful
millia = a thousand
Minerva = Minvera (in Greek = Athena)
minime = very, little, small
mino, are, avi, atus = drive
mirabilis, e = wonderful
miror, mirari, miratus = marvel
mirus, a, um= amazing
miser, misera, miserum = pitiable
mitto, mittere, misi, missus = send away
modernus, a, um = modern
mollius = easily
momentum, i (n) = moment
mons, montis (m) = mountain
Montana = Montana
mora, ae (f) = delay
motus, us (m) = (dance) move
mox = soon
multus, a, um = many
mundus, i (m) = world, universe
murus, muri (m) = wall
musso, are, avi, atus = mumble
muto, are, avi, atus = move, remove
mythicus, a, um = mythical
natura, ae (f) = nature

ne = negative
-ne = question word
necesse = necessary
Neptunus = Neptune (in Greek = Poseidon)
nihil = nothing
nolo, nolle, nolui = not wish
non = not
nos, nostrum/nostri, nobis, nos = we
noster, nostra, nostrum = our
novus, a, um = new
nullus, a, um = nothing, none
num = interrogative implies negative answer; whether
numerus, a, um = number
numquam = never
nuntia, ae (f) = female news anchor
nuntio, nuntiare, avi, atus (to announce) = broadcast, report
nuntius, a, um = message (substantively)
nuntius, i (m) = male news anchor
obsono, are, avi, atus = shop
occidentalis, e = western
occupo, are, avi, atus = occupy
oculus, i (m) = eye
offendo, offendere, offendi, offensus = hit (knock)
oliva, ae (f) = olive
Olympiae Ludis = the Olympic Games
Olympian = the Olympians, also known as Dii Consentes for their Roman counterparts
Olympus, i (m) = Olympus, home of the Olympians
omnis, e = everything
oportunitas, atis (f) = opportunity
optimus, a, um = best
opus, operis (n) = work
Oregone = Oregon
oro, orare, oravi, oratus = to speak
os, oris (n) = mouth
ostendo, ostendere, ostendi, ostentus = point out, show
Pacifici Oceano = the Pacific Ocean
paene = nearly, almost
paenitio, paenitere, paenitui = to be sorry
pagina, ae (f) = page
pando, are, avi, atus = spread, expand
Parisibus = Paris
paro, are, avi, atus = to prepare, make ready
paulisper = for a short while
paulus, a, um = little, small
pecunia, ae (f) = money
pello, pellere, pepuli, pulsus = drive away
per = through (+acc)

perdo, dere, didi, ditus = waste, lose
perficio, perficere, perfeci, perfectus = complete
perfluo, perfluere, perfluxi, perfluxus = flow
perplexa esse = bewildermnet
persuadeo, persuadere, persuasi, persuasus = persuade
pervenio, ire, veni, ventus = arrive
petasus, petasi (m) = hat
pluvia, ae (f) = rain
pono, ponere, posui, positus = put
popularis, e = popular
porto, are, avi, atus = carry
portus, us (m) = garage door
positio, onis (f) = position
possum, posse, potui = be able
post = after (+acc)
postmodum = after a while
postquam = after
praeparo, are, avi, atus = prepare
precor, precari, precatus = ask, beg
primus, a, um = first
princeps, principis = leader (substantively)
pro = for, on behalf (+abl)
probabilitier = probably
progredior, progredi, progressus sum = proceed
prope = near
propter = because of (+acc)
provincia, ae (f) = province, territory
proximus, a, um = next
prudens = foreknowing
pulcher, pulchra, pulchrum = beautiful
pulchritudo, inis (f) = beauty
pulsus, us (m) = blow, knock, hit
puto, are, avi, atus = think, suppose
quando = when?
quantus, a, um = amount
quattuordecim = fourteen
-que = and
queror, quereri, queri, questus sum = complain
qui, quae, quod = who, which what
quid = what
quippe = naturally, as expected
quod = because
quominus = that not, from
quomodo = in what way? how?
quotiens = whenever, as often as
rarus, a, um = rare
recedo, cedere, cessi, cessus = recede, step back
recipero, reciperare, avi, atus = recover
reclino, are, avi, atus = recline, lean back

regina, ae (f) = queen
rego, regere, rexi, rectus = guide, control
relinquo, linquere, liqui, lictus = abandon, leave
reliquus, a, um = remaining
reor, reri, ratus sum = think, suppose
requiesco, ere, requievi, requietus = recharge
res, rei (f) = affair, meeting
respondeo, spondere, spondi, sponsus = answer
resumo, resumere, resumpsi, resumptus = resume
retineo, tinere, tinui, tentus = hold back
revenio, revenire, reveni, reventus = return
rex, regis (m) = king
rideo, ridere, risi, risus = laugh at
rogo, are, avi, atus = ask
Roma, ae (f) = Rome
Romanus, i (m) = Roman
rursum = back
saepe = often
saepissime = frequent
salio, salire, salui, saltus = leap, jump
saluto, are, avi, atus = greet
salve, salvete = hello
sapientia, ae (f) = wisdom
satis, sat = sufficient, enough
scienter = knowingly, understandingly
scio, scire, scivi/ii, scitus = know
scribo, scribere, scripsi, scriptus = write
sed = but
sedeo, sedere, sedi, sessus = sit
senatus, us (m) = Senate
senex, is (m) = elder, senior
sentio, sentire, sensi, sensus = feel
serpens, entis (m) = snake
si = if
sic = thus, in this way
sicco, are, avi, atus = drain
sicut = just as, as
significio, are, avi, atus = signify (meant)
signum, i (n) = signal
silva, ae (f) = forest
similis, e = like, similar
sine = without (+abl)
sinistre, tra, trum = on the left
sol, solis (m) = the Sun
sollicito, are, avi, atus = worry
solus, a, um = alone
solutaris, solutaris (m) = shoe
solvo, solvere, solvi, solutus = solve
sonus, i (m) = noise, sound
soror, sororis (f) = sister
spectator, oris (m) = audience

specto, are, avi, atus = look at, consider
spiritus, us (m) = breath; spirit as in the Genie, from Aladdin, who grants three wishes to the person who rubs the magic lamp
splendidus, a, um = gorgeous
statim = immediatly
sternuo, sternuere, sternui = sneeze
stinguo, stinguere, - , - = extinguish
sto, stare, steti, status = stand
studeo, studere, studui = study (+dat)
studiosus, a, um = zealous
studium, i (n) = eagerness, zeal
stupor, oris (m) = stunned, amazement
suadeo, suadere, suasi, suasu = suggest
sub = under, close to (+acc or +abl)
subeo, subire, subii, subitus = go under
subito = suddenly
succedo, ere, cessi, cessus = succeed
sui, sibi, se, se = him-, her-, it-, themselves
sum, esse, fui, futurus = be, exist
summus, a, um = highest
super = over (+acc)
surrideo, ere, risi, risus = smile
tabesco, tabescere, tabui = evaporate
talem = such
talis, e = such, of such a kind
tam = so, so much
tamen = nevertheless, still
tandem = at last
tantus, a, um = so great, so much
tempestas, tempestatis (f) = weather
tempus, oris (n) = a period of time
tenebrosus, a, um = dark
teneo, tenere, tenui, tentus = to have, hold
tergeo, tergere, tersi, tersus = rub, wipe
terra, ae (f) = land
terreo, terrere, terrui, territus = frighten
territus, a, um = startled
togatus, a, um = wearing a toga
tollo, tollere, sustuli, sublatus = raise up
totius orbis = entire world
totus, a, um = entire
tremo, ere, ui = shake
trepide = restless, anxious
tres, tria = three
tridens, entis (m) = trident
tridens, ntis (n) = trident
triste = sadly
tui, tui, tibi, te = you
tum = then
turba, ae (f) = uproar
ubi = where, when
ubiquaque = in every place, wherever
ultimus, a, um = finally

umbrella, ae (f) = umbrella
undique = from all sides, everywhere
unus, a, um = one
urbs, urbis (f) = city
ut = as, so that
utilis, e = useful
utinam = if only! I wish!
venatio, onis (f) = hunting
venio, venire, veni, ventus = come
venor, venari, venatus = hunt
ventosus, a, um = windy
ventus, i (m) = wind
Venus = Venus (in Greek = Aphrodite)
verbum, i (n) = word
verto, vertere, verti, versus = turn
verus, a, um = original, real
Vesta = Vesta (in Greek = Hestia)
vestio, vestire, vestivi, vestitus = change clothes
vexamen, inis (n) = astonishment, shaking
vibro, are, avi, atus = rapidly shake
video, videre, vidi, visus = see
villa, ae (f) = house
vinco, vincere, vici, victus = win
vir, viri (m) = man
vis, vis (f) = power
visito, are, avi, atus = visit
voco, are, avi, atus = call, summon
volo, are, avi , atus = fly
voluntas, atis (f) = wish, desire
Vulcanus = Vulcan (in Greek = Hephaestus)
Washingtone = Washington

*the twelve gods and goddesses that make up the Olympians can also be referred to as Dii Consentes in Roman mythology